POPCORN

COOKBOOK

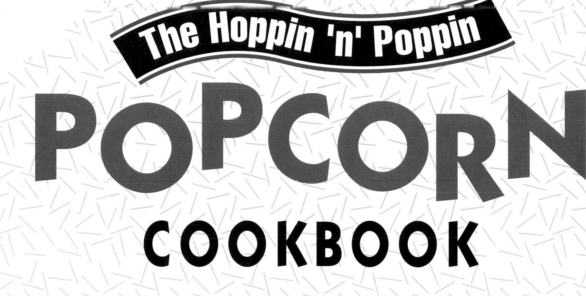

The Hoppin 'n' Poppin

POPCORN

COOKBOOK

Gina Steer

CHARTWELL
BOOKS, INC.

A QUINTET BOOK

Published by Chartwell Books
A Division of Book Sales, Inc.
PO Box 7100
Edison, New Jersey 08818-7100

ISBN 0-7858-0270-3

This book was designed and produced
by Quintet Publishing Limited
6 Blundell Street
London N7 9BH

Creative Director: Richard Dewing
Designer: Mark Roberts @ Design Revolution
Project Editors: Claire Tennant-Scull/Anna Briffa
Photographer: Jeremy Thomas
Food Stylist: Colin Capon

Typeset in Great Britain by
Central Southern Typesetters, Eastbourne
Manufactured in Malaysia by
C.H. Colour Scan Sdn. Bhd.
Printed in Singapore by
Star Standard Industries (Pte) Ltd

Acknowledgements:
The Publisher would like to thank
Swizzels Matlow Ltd for providing
products for photography.

contents

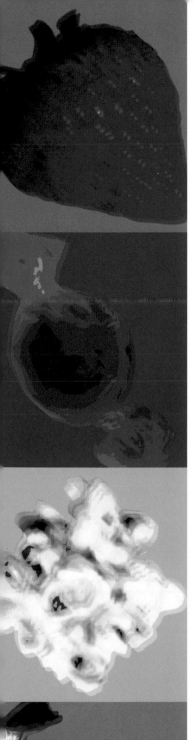

introduction

history

Most people think that popcorn is a modern food, but in fact it has been around for many centuries. The oldest ears of corn were found in Bat Cave, situated in west central Mexico. It was discovered that here the Cochise Indians, dating back to 2500 B.C., grew and ate popcorn. Scientists now believe that popcorn originated in Mexico. A funeral urn dated about A.D. 300 shows a maize god with some form of primitive popcorn in his head-dress. Preserved grains of popcorn that will still pop were found in tombs on the east coast of Peru, and are believed to be 1,000 years old.

the early popcorn

It was the original corn, wild and early cultivated, and the staple diet of the American Indian, that was used both for eating and decoration. At the first Thanksgiving feast in Plymouth, Massachusetts, one of the Chief's brothers arrived with goodwill gifts for the English colonists, of which one was a deerskin bag filled with popped popcorn.

After their introduction to popcorn, the colonists had the idea of eating popcorn with milk and sugar, and so breakfast cereal arrived. There were more than 700 varieties of popcorn grown at that time.

Columbus also found the natives in the West Indies eating popcorn as well as using it for decoration. When Cortes invaded Mexico in 1519, he discovered that popcorn was as important to the Aztecs as elsewhere, and was used for decorating their ceremonial head-dresses and necklaces, plus of course it was an integral part of their diet.

early methods of popping

The early consumers of popcorn popped it by toasting it over a fire, or even by throwing the cobs into the fire until the corn burst, although many tribes did use clay or metal cooking pots as well. It was the colonists who improved on the Indian cooking vessels and developed a corn popper that was made of thin sheet iron which revolved on an axle in front of the fire. Some of the corn popping vessels that are used in western and central Mexico today are direct descendants of these very early vessels. They are used with or without legs or lids, and do not necessarily need oil for popping.

Some of the popcorn was still popped on the cob, and the kernels remained attached. The Indians would pierce the center of the cob with a sharp stick, then toast on an open fire. These were an immensely popular snack.

It was in the 18th century that popping popcorn in oil really started, as it was discovered that it tasted much better than when simply toasted.

Popcorn is in fact corn, and although there are five different types of corn grown, popcorn is the only variety that pops. No variety of popcorn is the same, and it ranges in color from off-white to light gold, red, black and a variety of in-between colors.

Once popped, the corn has two basic shapes, snowflake which is large and shaped like a cumulus cloud, and mushroom, shaped like a large round ball.

nutritional value of popcorn

Popcorn is a combination of carbohydrate (principally starch), protein, fat and water. The water is stored in the small circle of soft starch.

Popcorn is not just a fun food; like other cereal grains it provides the body with heat and energy. It is now a recognized fact that the body needs about 4 ounces of carbohydrate a day in order to avoid the breakdown in body protein and other undesirable bodily changes. Apart from the carbohydrate content, popcorn is high in fiber and protein, and also contains phosphorous and iron. In its natural form, it has no artificial color, flavoring or additives, and is very low in calories. Four ounces of plain popped popcorn has only 27 calories, if tossed in butter about 126 calories.

Many health and medical groups feel that popcorn provides good nutritional benefits, and some weight-conscious groups recommend plain popcorn as a valuable substitute for other forms of carbohydrate. It also provides a valuable in-between meal snack if eaten plain as it satisfies the appetite without spoiling it.

why does popcorn pop?

When the kernel is heated, the water inside the kernel heats and the pressure builds up, causing the water to expand and the outer casing to burst. The kernel is then turned inside out, and the soft starch pops out as the steam inside is released.

It is down to personal choice whether you pop popcorn in a commercial electric popper, on the stove top, in the oven, open fire or even in a microwave.

If using a microwave, it is recommended that you use the popcorn that is sold specifically for microwaves; this is because of the packaging. As a microwave concentrates the heat on the largest item, the microwave popcorn is packed as densely as possible to insure maximum popability; this is best done by the packagers themselves, not by the average person popping corn.

If using an electric popper, follow the manufacturer's instructions. Never be tempted to overload the popper because you will not get a good result.

On the stove top, for each ¼ cup of unpopped popping corn use 2 tablespoons of oil. First heat the oil in a heavy-bottomed pan of at least 2½-quart capacity. Place on a high heat if using electricity or medium for gas. Heat to about 400°F. You can test the temperature by dropping one or two kernels into the oil. When the kernels spin in the oil, it is ready. You need enough to cover the base of the pan, certainly no more at any one time. When the oil has heated, add the corn kernels, and immediately cover with a tight-fitting lid. Shake or keep the pan moving constantly to make sure that each kernel is evenly coated with the oil. The corn will begin to pop within a few seconds. When the kernels have stopped popping, remove from the heat, and then wait for at least 1 minute before removing the lid. Discard any unpopped kernels, then coat with your favorite topping or mix.

old maids

If after popping you have any kernels that remain un-popped, discard them. The un-popped kernels are often referred to as Old Maids, and do not pop because they are too dry. However, they can be revived by placing them in a jar with water, securing with a tight-fitting lid and leaving for a couple of days, shaking occasionally.

Salt added to popcorn before popping results in tough popcorn, so always add it after popping.

storage

It is important to store popcorn properly. If popcorn is stored in the refrigerator, the moisture level can dry out and the popcorn will become soggy.

Store plain popcorn in an airtight container in a cool place or cabinet.

After popcorn has been mixed with a topping or mix, it is advisable to eat it the same day, and if the topping or mix is wet, within 2 to 3 hours.

Popcorn can be colored and used as decorations, by simply adding food coloring and a little water to the popped popcorn and shaking gently. This will provide fun decorations at parties for both children and adults. For the more adventurous, larger decorations can be fashioned using colored popcorn which would make a spectacular as well as fun centerpiece for any table.

consumption

Nowadays, most of the popcorn that is consumed is grown in the U.S.A. and although popular throughout the rest of the world, the consumption of popcorn is highest in the States. In 1992, 1,124,600,000 pounds of popcorn were consumed; this breaks down to 71 quarts per person.

Most of the popcorn is eaten in the home, and of that nearly all is home-popped, mainly with a salt, butter or toffee coating.

But that will become a thing of the past, now that popcorn is recognized as a fun, healthy food. There is a growing demand for many different varieties of toppings and mixes, and this book is packed full of tempting ideas that are quick'n'easy to prepare and cook. They provide a host of ideas for every conceivable occasion, and, unless otherwise stated, will serve four or more people as a generous appetizer.

Get popping – popcorn lovers!

11

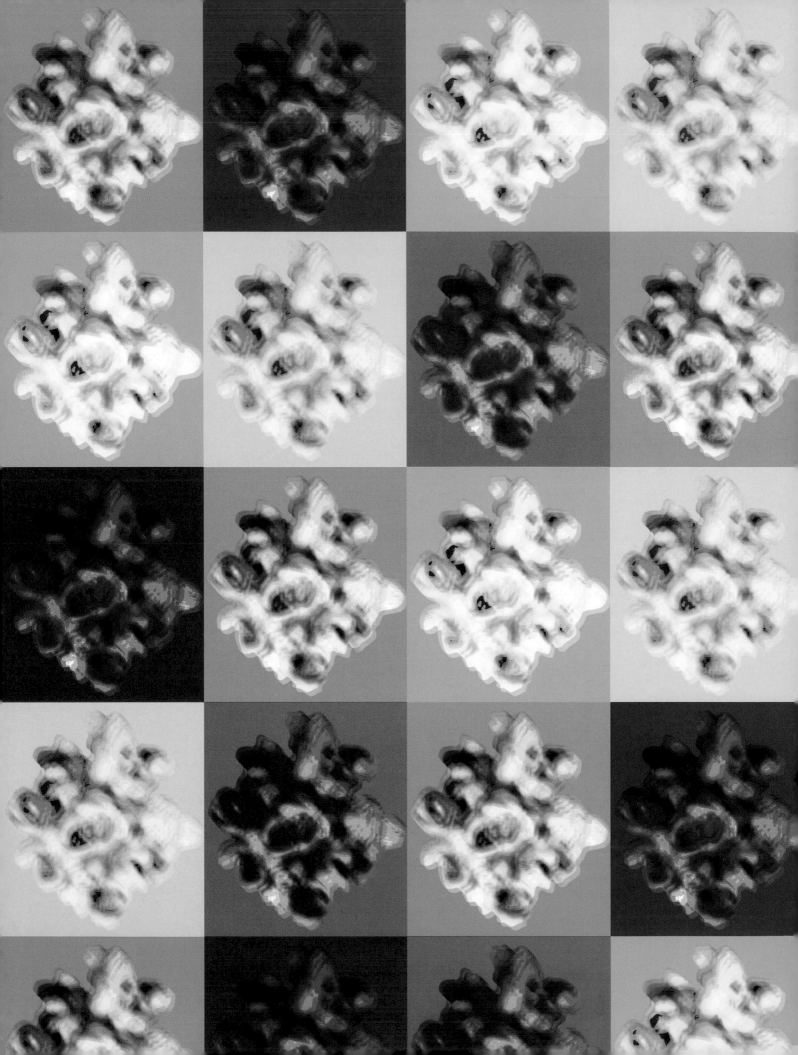

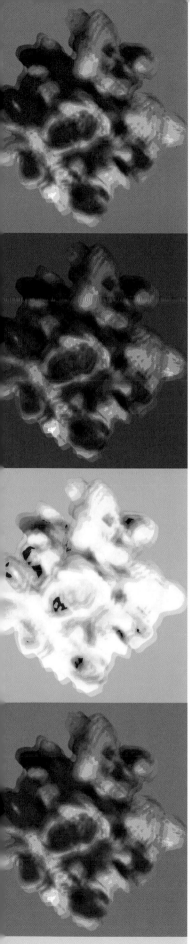

kids' treats

SALTY TEMPTER

**THE TRADITIONAL AND POSSIBLY
BEST-LOVED WAY OF EATING POPCORN.**

MAKES ABOUT 1 QUART

★ 2 tablespoons corn or
   groundnut oil
★ 2 tablespoons popping corn

FOR THE TOPPING

★ 1-1$\frac{1}{2}$ tablespoons coarsely
   milled kosher salt

Heat the oil in a large heavy-bottomed pan or "popper" and place over a medium heat if using gas, or a high heat if using an electric hot plate.

Add the popping corn, and cover with a tight-fitting lid. Shake gently.

Popping will start within 2 to 3 seconds, so keep the pan moving constantly by shaking it vigorously until the popping has completely stopped.

Remove the pan from the heat, but do not remove the lid for 1 minute. This will let any unpopped kernels pop in the residual heat.

Remove the lid, and pour the popcorn into a large bowl. Discard any unpopped kernels.

Coarsely grind the salt over the freshly popped popcorn and serve.

14

BUTTERY GOODIES

**THIS HAS TO BE MOST PEOPLE'S ALL-TIME
FAVORITE WAY OF EATING POPCORN.**

★ 1 quart freshly popped
   popcorn

FOR THE TOPPING

★ 3 tablespoons unsalted butter
★ pinch of salt

Pop the popcorn in a large heavy-bottomed pan as previously described, just before required.

Melt the butter in a large pan, and remove from the heat. Add the freshly popped popcorn and cover. Shake gently until the popcorn is completely coated, then sprinkle with salt to taste.

SALT

BUTTER

SuNNy-SIDe SaLAd MIx

**TRY SERVING THIS AS A
SALAD ACCOMPANIMENT AT A BARBECUE.**

★ 1 quart freshly popped popcorn
★ pinch of salt

FOR THE MIX

★ 2 ripe tomatoes, peeled, deseeded and finely chopped
★ 2-inch piece cucumber, peeled and finely chopped
★ 1 carrot, peeled and grated

★ 1 eating apple, cored and finely chopped
★ 1 tablespoon orange juice
★ 2 tablespoons freshly chopped mint
★ a few lettuce leaves, to serve

Pop the popcorn in a large heavy-bottomed pan as previously described, just before required. Sprinkle with salt to taste.

Place the tomatoes, cucumber and carrot in a mixing bowl. Toss the apple in the orange juice, then add to the tomatoes together with the mint. Mix together lightly.

Stir in the freshly popped popcorn and stir gently.

Arrange the lettuce leaves on individual serving plates, and top with the popcorn and tomato mix. Serve immediately.

16

TUNA TREAT

**IF PREFERRED, SERVE WITH
RAW VEGETABLE CRUDITÉS AND TACO CHIPS AS AN
UNUSUAL APPETIZER OR AT PARTIES.**

★ 1 quart freshly popped
popcorn

FOR THE TOPPING
★ 4 scallions, trimmed
and finely chopped
★ 2 celery stalks, trimmed

and finely chopped
★ 1 x $3^1/_2$ ounce can tuna,
drained and finely flaked
★ grated rind of 1 lemon
★ 1 tablespoon lemon juice
★ 3 tablespoons mayonnaise
★ scallion tassels, to garnish

Pop the popcorn in a large
heavy-bottomed pan as
previously described, just
before required.

Mix together the scallions,
celery, tuna and lemon rind and
juice. Stir in the mayonnaise.
Place the freshly popped
popcorn in a large mixing bowl,
and add the tuna mix.

Stir gently until the popcorn is
completely coated, and serve
immediately. Provide spoons or
forks for eating.

17

FiERy tEMPTEr

If Fresno chilies are unavailable,
you can use any other fresh chilies or even the jars
of freshly minced chili available in the supermarket. The amount
will depend on your heat tolerance, so start with a little
and increase according to taste.

★ 1 quart freshly popped
popcorn

FOR THE TOPPING

★ 1 small onion, peeled and
sliced
★ 2 cloves of garlic, peeled and
chopped

★ 2-3 Fresno red chili peppers,
deseeded and sliced
★ 2 tablespoons corn or
sunflower oil
★ 2 tablespoons freshly chopped
parsley
★ salt and freshly ground black
pepper

Pop the popcorn in a large
heavy-bottomed pan as
previously described, just
before required.

Place the onion, garlic and chili
in a pestle and mortar or food
processor fitted with a metal
blade, and either pound or
blend to a smooth purée.

Heat the oil in a skillet, and
gently sauté the purée for 5
minutes, stirring constantly.

Remove from the heat and stir
in the parsley and seasoning to
taste. Cool slightly.

Pour over the freshly
popped popcorn, and
stir gently until well
coated.

DUTCH SURPRISE

SERVE THIS WITH SALAD AND COLD MEATS AS A FUN, SNACK SALAD.

★ 1 quart freshly popped popcorn

FOR THE TOPPING

★ 2 tablespoons butter
★ 1 cup finely diced Edam or sharp Gouda cheese.
★ $\frac{1}{2}$-1 teaspoon ground mustard
★ 2 tablespoons freshly snipped chives

Pop the popcorn in a large heavy-bottomed pan as previously described, just before required.

Melt the butter in a pan, then add the cheese and ground mustard. Mix together lightly.

Add the freshly popped popcorn to the mix, and stir gently with a wooden spoon for 1 to 2 minutes, or until the popcorn is completely coated.

Sprinkle on the snipped chives and serve.

★ 19

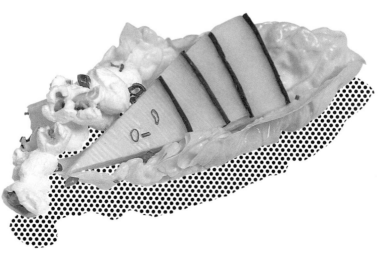

CRUNCHIE BRUNCH-TIME

**STUCK FOR AN IDEA FOR BRUNCH?
THEN LOOK NO FURTHER. THIS DISH WILL PROVIDE A HEALTHY AND
FILLING SNACK AND BRING A SMILE TO EVERYONE'S LIPS.**

★ 1 quart freshly popped popcorn

FOR THE TOPPING

★ 1 cup coarsely chopped, rindless bacon

★ 1 small onion, peeled and finely sliced
★ $\frac{2}{3}$ cup wiped and finely sliced mushrooms

Pop the popcorn in a large heavy-bottomed pan as previously described, just before required.

Put the bacon into a nonstick skillet, and place over a low heat. Cook slowly for 3 to 5 minutes, or until the fat begins to run out.

Increase the heat slightly, and add the onion. Cook, stirring frequently, for 5 minutes longer, or until the onion has softened. Stir in the mushrooms.

Increase the heat, and cook for 1 to 2 minutes longer, or until the bacon turns crisp.

Remove from the heat, and let cool before adding to the freshly popped popcorn. Stir gently until completely coated.

20

CHICKEN LICKIN'

FOR A CHANGE SUBSTITUTE TURKEY FOR THE CHICKEN MEAT. EITHER WAY, THIS POPCORN RECIPE IS LOW ON CALORIES, HIGH ON TASTE AND APPEAL.

★ 1 quart freshly popped popcorn

FOR THE TOPPING

★ 6 ounces boneless chicken breast

★ 1 tablespoon sunflower oil
★ 1 tablespoon butter
★ 1 tablespoon clear honey
★ grated rind of 1 small orange
★ 4 scallions, trimmed and finely chopped

Pop the popcorn in a large heavy-bottomed pan as previously described, just before required. Place in individual serving bowls.

Discard any skin from the chicken, and finely chop or cut into very thin shreds.

Heat the oil and butter in a large skillet, then add the chicken. Sauté for 3 to 5 minutes, or until sealed. Add the honey and orange rind, and cook for 5 minutes longer, or until the chicken is cooked and a light syrup has formed.

Remove from the heat, and stir in the scallions. Spoon the chicken mixture on top of the freshly popped popcorn, and serve immediately.

21

SAVORY DELIGHT

THIS SAVORY TOPPING IS GREAT FOR ALL AGES.

★ 1 quart freshly popped popcorn

FOR THE TOPPING

★ 1 tablespoon corn or
   sunflower oil

★ 2-3 teaspoons yeast extract

Pop the popcorn in a large heavy-bottomed pan as previously described, just before required.

Place the corn or sunflower oil and yeast extract in a large pan, and heat through, stirring constantly until well blended.

Remove from the heat, and let cool. Add the freshly popped popcorn to the pan.

Stir gently with a wooden spoon until the popcorn is completely coated in the topping.

until the popcorn is completely coated in the topping

22

HERBY DELIGHT

VARY THE HERBS ACCORDING TO AVAILABILITY AND PERSONAL PREFERENCE. FRESH HERBS ARE A MUST FOR THIS MIX, DRIED WILL NOT GIVE THE SAME TASTE AND AROMA.

★ 1 quart freshly popped popcorn

FOR THE MIX

★ 3 tablespoons virgin olive oil
★ 1 tablespoon freshly chopped basil
★ 1 tablespoon freshly chopped parsley
★ 1 tablespoon freshly chopped mint
★ pinch of salt

Pop the popcorn in a large heavy-bottomed pan as previously described, just before required.

Heat the oil in a large pan, and add the herbs. Gently sauté for 1 minute, stirring frequently.

Remove from the heat, and add to the freshly popped popcorn with a pinch of salt to taste. Stir gently with a wooden spoon. Alternatively, add the freshly popped popcorn to the pan, cover with a tight-fitting lid and shake gently.

When the popcorn is completely coated with the herbs, place in a serving bowl, and eat either warm or cold.

POPCORN STROGANOFF

IF YOU TRY SERVING THIS AS A VEGETARIAN ALTERNATIVE TO BEEF STROGANOFF, YOU MAY FIND THAT YOUR GUESTS SUDDENLY ALL TURN VEGETARIAN.

★ 1 quart freshly popped popcorn

FOR THE TOPPING

★ $2/3$ cup sour cream
★ 2 tablespoons freshly snipped chives
★ 1 large orange
★ $2/3$ cup wiped and finely chopped button mushrooms
★ $1/2$ cup finely grated sharp Cheddar cheese
★ salt and freshly ground black pepper

Pop the popcorn in a large heavy-bottomed pan as previously described, just before required.

Place the sour cream in a mixing bowl, and mix in the snipped chives.

Grate the rind from the orange, and divide the orange into segments, discarding the skin. Cut the segments into small pieces, then stir the rind and flesh into the sour cream together with the mushrooms. Add the cheese together with the seasoning and stir gently. Place the freshly popped popcorn in a large mixing bowl. Add the sour cream topping, and mix until the popcorn is completely coated. Serve.

★ 24

MIGHTY MEATIE

IF YOU LOVE BEEFY CHIPS, YOU'LL LOVE THIS POPCORN. YOU JUST WON'T BE ABLE TO EAT ENOUGH.

★ 1 quart freshly popped popcorn

FOR THE MIX

★ 2 tablespoons sunflower or corn oil
★ 1 tablespoon meat extract
★ $\frac{1}{2}$ teaspoon ground mustard

Pop the popcorn in a large heavy-bottomed pan as previously described, just before required.

Blend together the oil, meat extract and ground mustard, and place in a large pan.

Place over a low heat, and cook for 1 to 2 minutes, stirring once or twice or until blended. Remove from the heat. Add the freshly popped popcorn. Cover with a tight-fitting lid, and shake the pan vigorously for 1 minute, or until the popcorn is completely coated. Eat either warm or cold.

FISHY FUN

TRY SERVING THIS FUN TOPPING ON BAKED POTATOES, OR IN TACO SHELLS FILLED WITH SHREDDED LETTUCE.

★ 1 quart freshly popped popcorn

FOR THE TOPPING

★ 1 cup shelled shrimp, thawed if frozen
★ grated rind and juice of $\frac{1}{2}$ lemon
★ 4 scallions, trimmed and finely chopped
★ 1 eating apple, cored and finely chopped
★ salt and freshly ground black pepper
★ scant 1 cup fromage frais
★ 1 tablespoon tomato paste

Pop the popcorn in a large heavy-bottomed pan as previously described, just before required.

Drain the shrimp thoroughly, and gently squeeze out any excess moisture using paper towels. Finely chop and place in a mixing bowl.

Add the lemon rind and juice, the scallions and apple. Season to taste.

Blend the fromage frais with the tomato paste, and stir into the shrimp mixture.

Mix together well. Place on top of the freshly popped popcorn, and serve immediately.

25

HICKORY DICKORY

TRY SERVING THIS AT A COCKTAIL PARTY WITH A SELECTION OF OTHER NIBBLES. IT IS GUARANTEED TO BE EATEN FIRST.

★ 1 quart freshly popped
   popcorn

FOR THE MIX

★ 1 tablespoon sunflower or
   corn oil
★ $\frac{1}{2}$ cup whole walnuts or
   pecan nuts
★ 2-3 teaspoons hickory
   seasoning

Pop the popcorn in a large heavy-bottomed pan as previously described, just before required.

Heat the oil in a large heavy-bottomed pan, then sauté the nuts for 3 minutes, stirring frequently. Remove from the heat. Add the freshly popped popcorn and hickory seasoning, and cover with a tight-fitting lid.

Shake gently until the popcorn is completely coated, and place in small bowls. Serve.

26

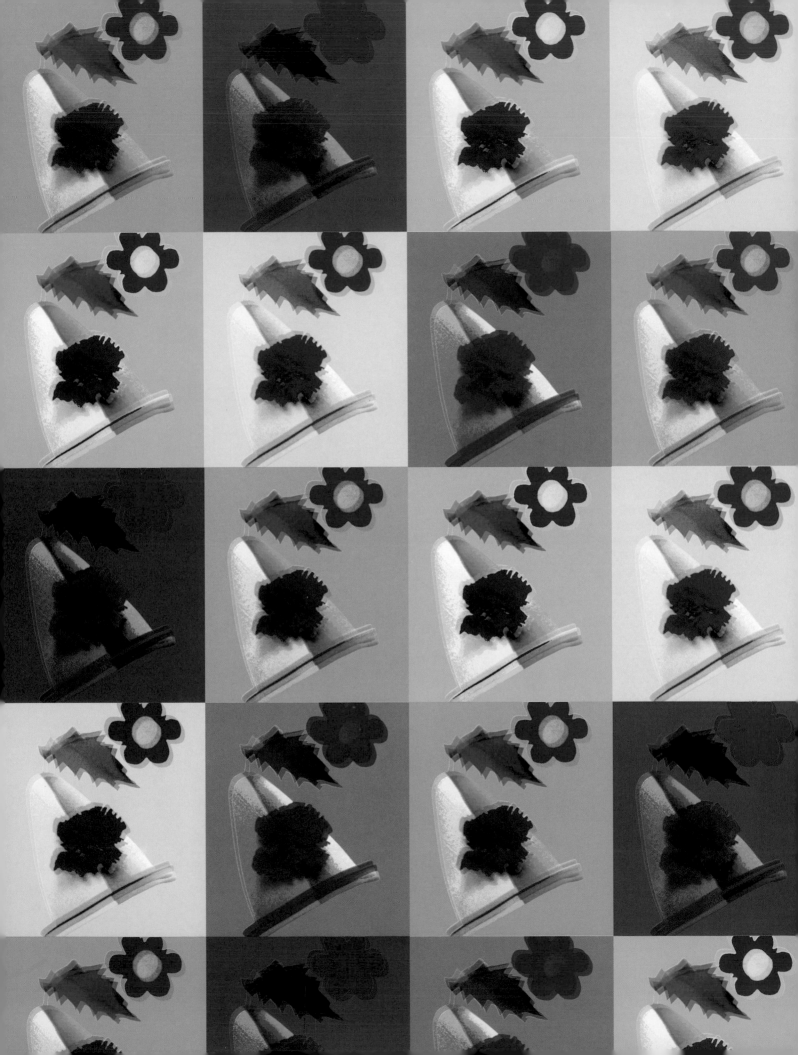

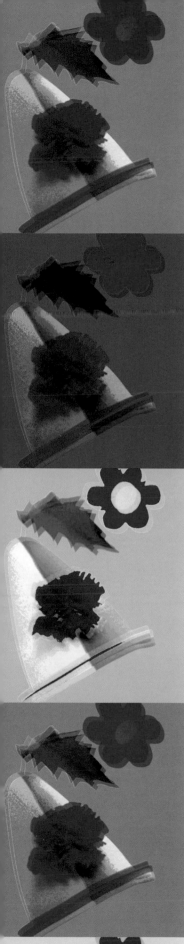

sophisticated savories

ITALIAN STYLE TOPPING

**IDEAL FOR SERVING AS A
PRE-DINNER APPETIZER.**

★ 1 quart freshly popped popcorn

FOR THE TOPPING

★ 3 tablespoons sunflower oil or reserved oil from the sun-dried tomatoes
★ 2 tablespoons butter

★ 8 sun-dried tomatoes in oil, drained and finely chopped
★ pinch of salt
★ $\frac{1}{2}$ teaspoon freshly ground black pepper
★ 2 tablespoons lemon juice
★ $\frac{1}{2}$ cup grated Parmesan cheese
★ 2 tablespoons freshly chopped basil

Pop the popcorn in a large heavy-bottomed pan as previously described, just before required.

Melt the butter and oil in a pan, then add the sun-dried tomatoes. Sauté gently for 5 minutes, or until the tomatoes are soft, stirring occasionally.

Add the seasoning, together with the lemon juice, Parmesan cheese and basil, and stir well. Remove from the heat and cool.

Add the freshly popped popcorn to the pan, cover with a tight-fitting lid and shake gently or stir gently with a wooden spoon until the popcorn is completely coated.

Place in a large serving bowl and serve.

30

COOL SALSA

SERVE THIS POPCORN AS A SNACK WITH TEQUILAS ON WARM SUMMER EVENINGS WHEN FRIENDS HAVE POPPED ROUND.

★ 1 quart freshly popped popcorn

FOR THE TOPPING

★ 1 small red bell pepper, deseeded, blanched and chopped
★ 2 ripe tomatoes, deseeded, peeled and finely chopped
★ 2-inch piece cucumber, peeled and finely chopped
★ 4 scallions, trimmed and finely chopped
★ grated rind and juice of 2 limes
★ 2 tablespoons freshly chopped cilantro
★ salt and freshly ground black pepper
★ celery stalks or taco chips, to serve

Pop the popcorn in a large heavy-bottomed pan as previously described, just before required.

Place the red bell pepper, tomatoes, cucumber and scallions in a mixing bowl.

Stir in the lime rind and juice, together with the cilantro. Season to taste. Place in a small mixing bowl, cover and leave for 30 minutes in the refrigerator for the flavors to develop.

Turn the freshly popped popcorn into a bowl. Spoon on the topping and stir gently. Serve with celery stalks or taco chips for scooping.

31

CARIBBEAN DREAM TOPPING

SERVE WITH A FEW GLASSES OF MALIBU – THEN RELAX, LIE BACK AND ENJOY THE SUN.

★ 1 quart freshly popped popcorn

FOR THE TOPPING

★ 1 small ripe papaya, deseeded, peeled and finely chopped
★ 2 tablespoons lime juice
★ 1 tablespoon molasses sugar
★ salt and cayenne pepper
★ 1-2 Scotch bonnet chili peppers, deseeded and finely chopped
★ or 1 teaspoon freshly minced chili peppers
★ $2/3$ cup freshly shaved coconut flesh or flakes
★ 1 tablespoon freshly chopped mint

Pop the popcorn in a large heavy-bottomed pan as previously described, just before required.

Place the chopped papaya, together with the lime juice, molasses sugar, seasoning, the chopped or minced chilies and the coconut flesh in a large mixing bowl.

Add the chopped mint, and stir the mixture well.

Add the freshly popped popcorn to the bowl, and stir gently with a wooden spoon until the popcorn is completely coated. Serve immediately.

TAPAS-STYLE POPCORN

SERVED WITH A VARIETY OF OTHER TAPAS-STYLE DISHES, THIS DISH WILL BE AN INSTANT HIT WITH ALL.

★ 1 quart freshly popped popcorn

FOR THE TOPPING

★ 3 tablespoons olive oil
★ $1/2$ Spanish onion, chopped
★ 2 cloves of garlic, crushed
★ 1 small yellow bell pepper, deseeded and finely chopped
★ 3 ounces chorizo sausage
★ 1 x 2-ounce can anchovy fillets, drained and chopped
★ $1/2$ cup pitted and roughly chopped black olives
★ salt and freshly ground black pepper
★ 2 tablespoons chopped parsley

Pop the popcorn in a large heavy-bottomed pan as previously described, just before required.

Heat the oil in a large pan, and gently sauté the onion and garlic for 5 minutes. Add the bell pepper, and sauté for 3 minutes longer.

Chop the chorizo sausage into small cubes, and add to the pan, together with the anchovies and chopped olives. Season to taste, and stir in the parsley. Heat through for 2 to 3 minutes, stirring occasionally.

Place the freshly popped popcorn into small serving bowls, and add the prepared topping to each. Serve immediately with chunks of bread.

32

CREAMY- BLUE CHEESY TOPPING

THERE ARE MANY VARIETIES OF BLUE CHEESE AVAILABLE, SOME CREAMY AND MILD, SOME STRONG AND CRUMBLY. TRY VARYING THE TYPE OF BLUE CHEESE IN THIS TOPPING TO GIVE A DIFFERENT FLAVOR AND TEXTURE.

★ 1 quart freshly popped popcorn

FOR THE TOPPING

★ $3/4$ cup crumbled Roquefort cheese
★ 2-3 tablespoons crème fraîche
★ 2 celery stalks, trimmed and finely chopped
★ 1 small onion, peeled and grated
★ $1/2$ cup finely chopped walnuts

Pop the popcorn in a large heavy-bottomed pan as previously described, just before required.

Place the cheese in a heavy-bottomed pan with the crème fraîche, and heat gently, stirring continuously until the cheese has melted.

Add the celery and onion, and continue to heat gently for 1 to 2 minutes.

Stir in the walnuts. Remove from the heat, and let cool. Add the freshly popped popcorn, and stir gently until the popcorn is completely coated. Serve immediately and eat with forks.

FRENCH- STYLE MIX

IF YOU LOVE GARLIC, THEN YOU'LL LOVE THIS MIX. FOR AN EXTRA SPECIAL TREAT, LOOK OUT FOR SMOKED GARLIC AND USE IT IN PLACE OF REGULAR GARLIC.

★ 1 quart freshly popped popcorn

FOR THE MIX

★ 3-4 cloves of garlic
★ 3 tablespoons virgin olive oil
★ 1 tablespoon freshly grated lemon rind
★ pinch of salt
★ 1 tablespoon freshly chopped parsley

Pop the popcorn in a large heavy-bottomed pan as previously described, just before required.

Peel the garlic and either chop very finely or crush. Heat the olive oil in a large pan, and gently sauté the garlic for 2 minutes, stirring frequently.

Add the lemon rind, salt and parsley, and heat through gently for 1 minute longer, stirring occasionally. Remove the pan from the heat, and let cool. Add the freshly popped popcorn to the pan, and cover with a tight-fitting lid. Shake vigorously – or stir with a wooden spoon until the popcorn is completely coated.

Place in individual serving bowls, and eat on the same day.

33

FIERY MEXICAN

THIS POPCORN IS FUN TO SERVE AS AN HORS D'OEUVRE IN PLACE OF A MORE TRADITIONAL RECIPE. REMEMBER TO TAKE GREAT CARE WHEN HANDLING RAW CHILIES.

★ 1 quart freshly popped popcorn

FOR THE TOPPING

★ 1 red bell pepper
★ 3 tablespoons sunflower or corn oil
★ 2-3 habanero red chili peppers, deseeded and finely chopped

★ 1 small onion, peeled and chopped
★ 2 cloves of garlic, peeled and crushed
★ 1 small ripe, firm avocado
★ grated rind and juice of $\frac{1}{2}$ lemon
★ 2 tablespoons freshly chopped flat-leaf parsley
★ salt and freshly ground black pepper

Pop the popcorn in a large heavy-bottomed pan as previously described, just before required.

Preheat the broiler. Cut the red bell pepper in half, and discard the seeds. Place skin-side uppermost on the broiler rack sitting in the broiler pan. Pour over 2 tablespoons of the oil, then cook, for about 10 minutes or until the skins have blistered and blackened. Take care not to burn the pepper. Remove from the heat, and let cool before peeling. Discard the skin. Chop into strips and reserve until needed.

Heat the remaining oil in a pan, and sauté the chopped chilies, onion and garlic for 5 minutes, stirring occasionally.

Add the chopped pepper and continue to heat through for 1 minute longer.

Peel the avocado and discard the pit. Chop the flesh into small dice, and toss in the lemon juice.

Add to the pan with the lemon rind and herbs, and season to taste. Heat through, stirring occasionally for 2 to 3 minutes, or until hot.

Place the freshly popped popcorn in a serving bowl. Top with the chili and avocado topping, and serve immediately.

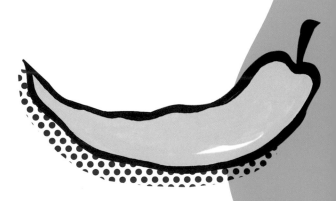

'COOL MON'

JAMAICAN HOT PEPPER SAUCE IS GROWING IN POPULARITY. IF USING FOR THE FIRST TIME, TAKE CARE; IT'S A SERIOUSLY HOT SAUCE AND IS CERTAINLY NOT INTENDED FOR THE FAINT-HEARTED.

★ 1 quart freshly popped popcorn

FOR THE MIX

★ 3 tablespoons butter
★ pinch of salt
★ 2 tablespoons paprika pepper
★ few shakes of Jamaican Hot Pepper sauce, to taste

Pop the popcorn in a large heavy-bottomed pan as previously described, just before required.

Melt the butter in a large pan, and remove from the heat. Add the salt, paprika pepper, Hot Pepper sauce and the freshly popped popcorn.

Cover the pan with a tight-fitting lid, and shake vigorously for 1 minute, or stir with a wooden spoon until the popcorn is completely coated. Serve warm or cold.

36

HOT'N'SPICY

TRY THIS TOPPING OVER POPCORN AT THE START OF AN INDIAN MEAL WITH SOME LONG COOL BEERS.

- ★ 1 quart freshly popped popcorn

FOR THE TOPPING

- ★ 2 tablespoons sunflower or corn oil
- ★ 1 onion, peeled and finely chopped
- ★ 2 cloves of garlic, peeled and crushed
- ★ 2-3 green chili peppers, deseeded and chopped
- ★ 2 teaspoons freshly minced ginger root
- ★ 1 teaspoon ground coriander
- ★ 1 teaspoon ground cumin
- ★ 1 teaspoon ground cinnamon
- ★ 1 teaspoon fenugreek seeds, crushed
- ★ $\frac{1}{2}$ teaspoon turmeric
- ★ $\frac{2}{3}$ cup natural yogurt
- ★ 2 tablespoons cilantro leaves, to garnish

Pop the popcorn in a large heavy-bottomed pan as previously described, just before required.

Heat the oil in a skillet, then sauté the onion, garlic and chilies for 3 minutes.

Add the ginger and spices, and sauté for 3 minutes longer over a gentle heat, stirring occasionally. Stir in the yogurt, and cook for 2 to 3 minutes, stirring frequently.

Sprinkle with the cilantro, and mix well. Remove from the heat, and let cool.

SAUCY TAVERNA POPCORN

ZORBA WOULD NEVER HAVE STOPPED DANCING IF HE HAD EATEN A FEW BOWLS OF THIS!

★ 1 quart freshly popped popcorn

FOR THE TOPPING

★ 1 red onion, peeled and sliced

★ 1 cup feta cheese, cut into cubes

★ 2 tomatoes, peeled and finely sliced

★ $\frac{1}{2}$ cup pitted, whole black olives

★ $\frac{2}{3}$ cup Greek-style yogurt

★ 1 tablespoon freshly chopped mint

★ warm pocket bread, to serve

Pop the popcorn in a large heavy-bottomed pan as previously described, just before required.

Place the onion in a mixing bowl, together with the feta cheese, tomatoes and olives.

Stir in the yogurt and mint. Mix together well. Place the freshly popped popcorn into a serving dish, and spoon over the topping. Stir gently until the popcorn is completely coated.

Serve immediately with warm pocket bread cut into strips to use as scoops.

38

FRAGRANT MIX

WARM SAKI IS A MUST TO SERVE WITH THESE LITTLE MORSELS.

★ 1 quart freshly popped popcorn

FOR THE MIX

★ 3 lemon grass stalks
★ 1 Thai red chili pepper, deseeded
★ 3 tablespoons sunflower or corn oil
★ 1 teaspoon freshly minced ginger root
★ 1 tablespoon soy sauce
★ 1 tablespoon lime juice
★ $\frac{1}{2}$ cup grated fresh coconut flesh

Pop the popcorn in a large heavy-bottomed pan as previously described, just before required.

Remove the outer leaves from the lemon grass, and chop the lemon grass and chili very finely.

Heat the oil in a medium-sized pan, and gently sauté the lemon grass, chili, and ginger for 3 minutes, stirring frequently.

Add the soy sauce and lime juice, and cook for 30 seconds longer. Remove from the heat, and let cool slightly. Add the freshly popped popcorn and coconut, and cover with a tight-fitting lid. Shake or stir gently with a wooden spoon until the popcorn is completely coated. Eat warm or cold.

MADRAS-STYLE POPCORN

DON'T BE TEMPTED TO CHEAT AND JUST USE CURRY POWDER, THE FLAVOR JUST WON'T BE THE SAME.

★ 1 quart freshly popped popcorn

FOR THE MIX

★ 2 tablespoons sunflower or corn oil
★ 2 cloves of garlic, peeled and crushed
★ 1-2 Thai chili peppers, deseeded and chopped
★ 1-2 teaspoons chili powder
★ 3 teaspoons garam masala
★ 1 tablespoon tomato paste
★ 1 tablespoon lemon juice

Pop the popcorn in a large, heavy-bottomed pan as previously described, just before required.

Heat the oil in a large pan, and sauté the garlic and the chilies for 3 minutes.

Add the chili powder and garam masala, and sauté gently for 3 minutes longer, stirring frequently.

Blend the tomato paste with the lemon juice, and stir into the spice mix. Cook for 30 seconds. Remove the pan from the heat, and let cool slightly.

Add the freshly popped popcorn. Cover with a tight-fitting lid, and shake or stir gently with a wooden spoon until the popcorn is completely coated with the mix.

40

TRAIL MIX

**IF YOU'RE WATCHING YOUR CALORIES,
TRY THIS HEALTHY ALTERNATIVE TO THE BUTTERY OR SWEET TOPPINGS.**

★ 1 quart freshly popped
popcorn

FOR THE MIX

★ grated rind of 2 oranges

★ $\frac{1}{2}$ cup finely chopped
no-need-to-soak apricots
★ $\frac{1}{2}$ cup finely chopped
no-need-to-soak prunes
★ $\frac{1}{2}$ cup toasted sesame seeds
★ $\frac{1}{2}$ cup toasted pumpkin seeds

Pop the popcorn in a large heavy-bottomed pan as previously described. While still in the pan, add the grated orange rind. Cover with a tight-fitting lid, and shake vigorously until the popcorn is completely coated with the rind.

Add the remaining ingredients to the freshly popped popcorn, and mix together well. Eat the same day.

NUTTY TREASURE MIX

SQUIRRELS WON'T BE THE ONLY LOVERS OF THESE NIBBLES. KIDS OF ALL AGES WILL GO "NUTS" OVER THIS POPCORN!

* 1 quart freshly popped popcorn

FOR THE MIX

* 2 tablespoons olive oil
* $\frac{1}{2}$ cup pine nuts

* $\frac{1}{2}$ cup roughly chopped pecan nuts
* $\frac{3}{4}$ cup chopped candied pineapple
* $\frac{2}{3}$ cup dried coconut flakes

Pop the popcorn in a large heavy-bottomed pan as previously described, just before required.

Heat the oil in a pan, and gently sauté the pine nuts for 2 to 3 minutes, or until lightly toasted. Add the chopped pecan nuts for the last minute.

Remove from the heat, and stir in the remaining ingredients except the freshly popped popcorn. Cool slightly, then add the popcorn. Stir gently with a wooden spoon to make sure that the ingredients are well mixed. Eat the same day, or store in airtight containers.

42

PESTO SURPRISE

**YOU CAN USE A PESTLE AND MORTAR
TO MAKE THE PESTO IF PREFERRED. HOWEVER, WHICHEVER WAY
YOU CHOOSE, EAT ON THE SAME DAY.**

★ 1 quart freshly popped
  popcorn

FOR THE MIX

★ 1 tablespoon fresh basil leaves
★ 1 clove of garlic, peeled and
  crushed

★ $\frac{1}{4}$ cup pine nuts
★ 4 tablespoons olive oil
★ 1 tablespoon freshly grated
  Parmesan cheese
★ pinch of salt
★ freshly shaved Parmesan

Pop the popcorn in a large
heavy-bottomed pan as
previously described, just
before required.

Place the basil, garlic and pine
nuts in a food processor, and
blend to form a purée, slowly
pouring in the oil while the
machine is still running.

Place the purée in a bowl, and
stir in the cheese and salt.

Let the freshly popped popcorn
cool in the pan, then add the
pesto sauce.

Stir gently with a wooden spoon
to coat popcorn. Add Parmesan
shavings and serve.

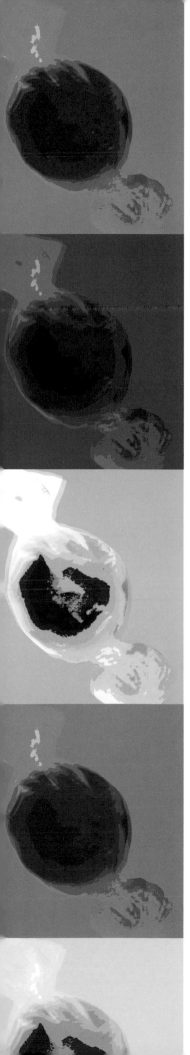

Chapter Three

sweet ideas

CHOCOHOLICS

**IF YOU'RE A CHOCOHOLIC,
THEN THIS FUN-FLAVORED POPCORN IS A
MUST FOR YOU.**

★ 1 quart freshly popped
popcorn

FOR THE MIX

★ 4 squares dark chocolate
★ 2 tablespoons butter
★ 3 tablespoons light corn syrup

Pop the popcorn in a large heavy-bottomed pan as previously described, just before required.

Break the chocolate into small pieces, and place in a large heavy-bottomed pan, together with the butter and syrup.

Place over a gentle heat, and let the mixture melt, stirring occasionally with a wooden spoon.

When the chocolate has melted, bring to a boil, and boil steadily for 1 minute.

Remove from the heat, and add the freshly popped popcorn, stirring gently with a wooden spoon until the popcorn is completely coated. Let cool. Eat the same day.

If desired, sprinkle with grated white chocolate.

46

SMOOTHIE FRUITY POPS

**IF PEANUT BUTTER IS YOUR FORTE,
YOU'LL LOVE THIS MIX. LOOK OUT FOR JARS OF PEANUT BUTTER AND
JELLY IN YOUR LOCAL SUPERMARKET.**

★ 1 quart freshly popped popcorn

FOR THE MIX

★ 2 tablespoons smooth peanut butter with jelly

★ 3 tablespoons light corn syrup
★ $3/4$ cup finely chopped no-need-to-soak prunes
★ 2-3 tablespoons heavy cream

Pop the popcorn in a large heavy-bottomed pan as previously described, just before required.

Place the peanut butter with jelly and the syrup in a large pan, and heat gently until melted, stirring occasionally.

Bring to a boil, and simmer for 1 minute. Remove from the heat, and stir in the prunes and cream. Return to the heat, and heat for 30 seconds longer, stirring continuously. Remove from the heat again, and let cool for about 1 minute.

Add the freshly popped popcorn, and stir until it is completely coated.

Turn into a serving dish and serve. Eat the same day.

MALLOW DELIGHT

IDEAL FOR THOSE WITH A SWEET AND FRUITY PALATE.

★ 1 quart freshly popped popcorn

FOR THE MIX

★ 4 ounces marshmallows
★ 2 tablespoons butter
★ 2 tablespoons milk
★ $\frac{1}{2}$ cup chopped candied cherries
★ $\frac{1}{4}$ cup chopped angelica

Pop the popcorn in a large heavy-bottomed pan as previously described, just before required.

Chop half the marshmallows into small pieces, and reserve for mixing into the popcorn with the cherries.

Place the remaining marshmallows with the butter and milk in a heavy-bottomed pan, and heat gently until the marshmallows have melted. Stir until smooth.

Add the chopped candied cherries, remaining marshmallows and angelica and stir together well. Remove from the heat, and let cool. Add the freshly popped popcorn, and stir gently. Place in bowls and serve.

NUTTY BITES

**YOU'LL GO CRAZY FOR THIS POPCORN.
ONCE YOU START EATING IT, YOU JUST WON'T BE ABLE TO STOP —
IT'S DEFINITELY VERY, VERY MOREISH.**

★ 1 quart freshly popped popcorn

FOR THE MIX

★ $\frac{1}{2}$ cup granulated sugar

★ $\frac{1}{2}$ cup whole, shelled pistachio nuts
★ $\frac{1}{2}$ cup toasted, flaked almonds
★ a few drops of almond extract

Pop the popcorn in a large heavy-bottomed pan as previously described, just before serving.

Dissolve the sugar in a heavy-bottomed pan with ⅔ cup of water over a gentle heat, stirring occasionally. When the sugar has melted, bring to a boil, and cook for 3 minutes or until a light syrup has formed.

Remove from the heat, and stir in the nuts and almond extract. Let cool slightly.

Gently stir in the freshly popped popcorn, and let cool a little before eating.

50

YANKEE DOODLE TREAT

BRIBE THE KIDS WITH THIS DESSERT, IT WILL GUARANTEE CLEAN PLATES.

★ 1 quart freshly popped popcorn

FOR THE TOPPING

★ 2 tablespoons smooth peanut butter
★ 2 tablespoons light corn syrup

★ 2-3 tablespoons heavy cream
★ ice cream, to serve
★ chocolate sugar strands, to decorate

Pop the popcorn in a large heavy-bottomed pan as previously described, just before required.

Place the peanut butter and syrup in a large heavy-bottomed pan and heat, stirring occasionally, until the peanut butter has melted.

Bring to a boil, and simmer for 1 minute, then stir in the cream. Cook for 30 seconds, and remove from the heat. Cool slightly, then add the freshly popped popcorn and stir gently with a wooden spoon until completely coated.

Place scoops of ice cream in serving bowls, top with the peanut butter popcorn and serve sprinkled with chocolate sugar strands.

MOCHA MAGIC

IF YOU LOVE CAPPUCCINO, THIS POPCORN IS A MUST.

★ 1 quart freshly popped popcorn

FOR THE MIX

★ 3 squares dark chocolate
★ 1 tablespoon very strong black coffee
★ 1 tablespoon butter
★ 2 tablespoons heavy cream
★ 2 teaspoons sifted cocoa powder

Pop the popcorn in a large heavy-bottomed pan as previously described, just before required.

Break the chocolate into a large heavy-bottomed pan, and add the coffee and butter.

Melt over a gentle heat, stirring occasionally until smooth. Add the cream, and cook gently for 1 minute longer.

Remove from the heat, and let cool slightly. Gently stir in the freshly popped popcorn. Keep stirring until the popcorn is completely coated.

Remove from the heat, and place in serving containers. Serve sprinkled with the sifted cocoa powder.

TOFFEE POPS

KIDS WILL LOVE THIS POPCORN AND IT WILL BECOME A BIG HIT AT PARTIES OR WHEN THEY RETURN HOME FROM SCHOOL.

★ 1 quart freshly popped popcorn

FOR THE MIX

★ 2 tablespoons butter
★ 2 tablespoons light corn syrup
★ $\frac{1}{3}$ cup dark soft brown sugar
★ $\frac{1}{4}$ cup heavy cream

Pop the popcorn in a large heavy-bottomed pan as previously described, just before required.

Melt the butter, syrup and sugar in a large heavy-bottomed pan over a gentle heat, stirring occasionally with a wooden spoon until blended.

Add the cream, stirring all the time. Bring to a boil, and remove from the heat just as it reaches boiling point.

Cool slightly, then add the freshly popped popcorn. Stir gently until completely coated. Serve warm or cold.

53

SYRUPY AFTERTHOUGHTS

TRY PUTTING SMALL SPOONFULS INTO PETITS FOURS CASES AND SERVING AFTER DESSERT. JUST WATCH THE FAMILY'S EYES LIGHT UP.

★ 1 quart freshly popped popcorn

FOR THE MIX

★ 4 tablespoons light corn syrup
★ 2 tablespoons butter

★ 1 tablespoon sifted cocoa powder
★ a few drops of vanilla extract
★ $\frac{3}{4}$ cup roughly chopped pecan nuts

Pop the popcorn in a large heavy-bottomed pan as previously described, just before required.

Melt the syrup, butter and cocoa powder in a heavy-bottomed pan over a gentle heat, stirring occasionally with a wooden spoon until blended.

When the syrup has melted, bring to a boil, and cook for 1 minute. Remove from the heat, and stir in the vanilla extract and nuts.

Let cool slightly, then stir in the freshly popped popcorn. Stir gently until the popcorn is completely coated, and place in containers or bowls. Eat on the same day.

54

SHOOFLY PUFF

**COME DOWN TO THE DEEP SOUTH AND
GET A TASTE OF SHEER HEAVEN.**

★ 1 quart freshly popped popcorn

FOR THE MIX

★ $1/2$ cup molasses sugar
★ 2 tablespoons butter

★ 1 teaspoon ground cinnamon
★ $1/2$ teaspoon freshly grated nutmeg
★ $1/2$ teaspoon ground ginger
★ 3 tablespoons heavy cream

Pop the popcorn in a large heavy-bottomed pan as previously described, just before required.

Place the sugar, butter and spices in a large heavy-bottomed pan, and heat gently, stirring frequently until the sugar and butter have melted.

Add the cream, and stir well. Bring to just below boiling point. Remove from the heat, and let cool slightly. Add the freshly popped popcorn, and stir well until it is completely coated. Spoon into serving bowls, and eat the same day.

MINTY POPS

SERVE THIS FUN-FLAVORED POPCORN AFTER DINNER AS A DIFFERENT KIND OF PETITS FOURS.

★ 1 quart freshly popped popcorn

FOR THE MIX

★ $1/_3$ cup granulated sugar

★ 2 tablespoons crème de menthe
★ 2 ounces crème de menthe-flavored Turkish creams

Pop the popcorn in a large heavy-bottomed pan as previously described, just before required.

Melt the sugar with ⅔ cup of water in a large heavy-bottomed pan. Bring to a boil, and boil steadily for 3 minutes, or until a light sugar syrup has formed.

Remove from the heat, and stir in the crème de menthe. Let cool slightly.

Chop the crème de menthe-flavored Turkish creams into small pieces, and add to the pan together with the freshly popped popcorn. Stir gently until completely coated.

Place in small serving dishes, and eat the same day.

BOOZY CHOCS

FOR SERIOUS DEVOTEES OF POPCORN AND CHOCOLATE.

★ 1 quart freshly popped popcorn

FOR THE MIX

★ 4 squares dark chocolate

★ 2 tablespoons butter
★ 2 tablespoons light cream
★ $1/_3$ cup raisins
★ 2 tablespoons rum

Pop the popcorn in a large heavy-bottomed pan as previously described, just before required.

Break the chocolate into small pieces, and place in a large heavy-bottomed pan together with the butter and cream. Melt over a gentle heat, stirring

occasionally until smooth. When melted, cook for 1 minute. Remove from the heat. Add the raisins and rum, and stir well. Let cool slightly. Add the freshly popped popcorn, and stir until completely coated.

Place in serving bowls, and eat on the same day.

GINGERED CRISP

**PEP UP YOUR PALATE WITH
THIS CRUNCHY TOPPING.**

★ 1 quart freshly popped popcorn

FOR THE MIX

★ 4 ounces gingersnap cookies

★ 2 tablespoons butter
★ 3 tablespoons light corn syrup
★ $\frac{1}{4}$ cup chopped candied ginger

Pop the popcorn in a large heavy-bottomed pan as previously described, just before required.

Roughly crush the cookies into bite-sized pieces, and reserve.

Heat the butter and syrup in a heavy-bottomed pan, then stir continuously until melted. Remove from the heat, and let cool slightly. Then stir in the crushed cookies and freshly popped popcorn. Stir gently with a wooden spoon, taking care not to crush the cookies any more. Sprinkle with the candied ginger. Eat the same day.

Chapter Four

4

fruity afterthoughts

Apricot Melba

A very original version of the classic dish that is universally popular. This one will become even more popular.

* 1 quart freshly popped popcorn

FOR THE TOPPING

* 3 cups fresh raspberries
* 1 tablespoon lemon juice

* 4-$4\frac{1}{2}$ tablespoons sifted confectioners' sugar or to taste
* 2 teaspoons arrowroot
* $\frac{1}{2}$-$\frac{3}{4}$ cup no-need-to-soak dried apricots

Pop the popcorn in a large heavy-bottomed pan as previously described, just before required.

Pick over the raspberries, and place in a blender, together with the lemon juice and sugar. Blend to form a smooth purée. Pass through a fine strainer to remove the seeds, then place in a pan and bring to a boil.

Blend the arrowroot to a smooth paste with 2 tablespoons of water, and stir into the raspberry purée. Cook, stirring, for 2 to 3 minutes, or until the purée has thickened. Remove from the heat, and let the purée cool slightly.

Chop the apricots into small pieces, and stir into the raspberry purée, together with the freshly popped popcorn. Stir until lightly coated. Eat the same day.

CALYPSO

TRY A TRUE TASTE OF THE CARIBBEAN WITH THIS FRUITY MANGO TOPPING. SERVE AS A TOPPING FOR ICE CREAM.

★ 1 quart freshly popped popcorn

FOR THE TOPPING

★ 1 ripe mango, peeled, pit removed and finely chopped

★ 1 small fresh pineapple, skinned, cored and finely diced

★ grated rind of 1 lime

★ 1-2 tablespoons clear honey, warmed

★ $\frac{2}{3}$ cup coconut flakes

★ $\frac{1}{2}$ cup roasted cashew nuts

Pop the popcorn in a large heavy-bottomed pan as previously described, just before required.

Place the chopped mango flesh, pineapple, lime rind, honey, coconut flakes and cashew nuts in a large mixing bowl. Mix in the freshly popped popcorn, and stir gently with a wooden spoon until lightly coated.

Place in a serving dish lined with pineapple leaves, and serve.

61

TASTE OF THE TROPICS

**YOU CAN VARY THE DRIED AND CANDIED FRUITS
USED IN THIS TOPPING ACCORDING TO YOUR OWN PERSONAL
TASTE AND AVAILABILITY OF THE FRUITS.**

★ 1 quart freshly popped
   popcorn

FOR THE TOPPING
★ $3/4$ cup ready-chopped dates
★ $1/2$ cup washed, dried and
   chopped candied cherries
★ $1/3$ cup golden raisins

★ $1/2$ cup toasted slivered
   almonds
★ $1/2$ cup banana chips
★ 3 tablespoons light corn syrup
★ 2 tablespoons melted butter

Place the dates, cherries, golden raisins, almonds and banana chips together in a mixing bowl, and reserve.

Pop the popcorn in a large heavy-bottomed pan as previously described. When the popcorn has finished popping, add the syrup and butter. Cover the pan with a tight-fitting lid, and shake the pan or stir gently until the popcorn is completely coated.

Add the reserved fruit mixture, and either cover and shake the pan, or stir gently with a wooden spoon until the fruit mixture is evenly distributed throughout.

Serve and eat on the same day.

62

TANGY LEMON MERINGUE

**WHEN MAKING MERINGUE, IT IS ALWAYS
A GOOD IDEA TO MAKE A LITTLE EXTRA SO THAT IT CAN BE USED TO MAKE
LITTLE TINY MERINGUES WHICH ARE IDEAL AS ACCOMPANIMENTS FOR
FRUIT DESSERTS, ICE CREAM OR WITH THIS TOPPING.**

★ 1 quart freshly popped popcorn

FOR THE TOPPING

★ 3-4 medium-size prepared meringues

★ grated rind and juice of 1 large lemon
★ 2 tablespoons sugar or to taste
★ 1 tablespoon cornstarch
★ 2 teaspoons butter

Pop the popcorn in a large heavy-bottomed pan as previously described, just before required.

Crush the meringues lightly or break into pieces, and reserve.

Place the lemon rind and juice, made up to ½ cup with water, in a large pan with the sugar. Bring to a boil, stirring occasionally.

Blend the cornstarch to a smooth paste with 2 tablespoons of water, then stir into the boiling liquid. Cook, stirring continuously, for 2 minutes, or until thickened.

Remove from the heat, and add the butter, stirring until melted. Let cool slightly, then add the freshly popped popcorn and crushed meringues. Stir gently until the popcorn and meringues are completely coated, then serve.

63

CHIP CHOC

LOOK OUT FOR DIFFERENT FLAVORED CHOCOLATE CHIPS. THEY ARE AVAILABLE IN DARK, MILK AND WHITE.

★ 1 quart freshly popped popcorn

FOR THE MIX
★ $\frac{1}{3}$ cup dark chocolate chips
★ $\frac{1}{3}$ cup milk chocolate chips
★ 2 tablespoons white chocolate chips
★ $\frac{1}{2}$ cup dried banana chips
★ 3 tablespoons light corn syrup

Place all the chocolate and banana chips in a mixing bowl, and reserve.

Pop the popcorn in a large heavy-bottomed pan as previously described. When the corn has finished popping, add the syrup.

Heat through for 1 minute, and cover the pan with a tight-fitting lid. Shake vigorously, or stir with a wooden spoon.

Add the reserved chocolate chips and banana chips, and mix lightly. Eat on the same day.

KEY LIME

A VARIATION OF THE FAMOUS KEY LIME PIE THAT ORIGINATED FROM KEY WEST IN FLORIDA, THIS ONE HOWEVER CAN BE NIBBLED ANY TIME, DAY OR NIGHT.

★ 1 quart freshly popped popcorn

FOR THE MIX
★ $\frac{2}{3}$ cup condensed milk
★ 2 tablespoons butter
★ juice and grated rind of 2 limes
★ 3-4 medium-size prepared meringues, lightly crushed

Pop the popcorn in a large heavy-bottomed pan as previously described, just before required.

Place the condensed milk and butter in a heavy-bottomed pan. Bring to a boil, stirring frequently, then reduce the heat, and simmer gently for 5 minutes, again stirring frequently. Remove from the heat, and stir in the lime juice and rind. Let cool slightly, then stir in the freshly popped popcorn and lightly crushed meringue.

Stir gently until completely coated. Leave until cold before eating.

REDCURRANT AND PORT

SERVE THIS POPCORN AT THANKSGIVING AS AN APPETIZER TO THE THANKSGIVING MEAL, BUT MAKE SURE YOUR GUESTS DON'T EAT SO MUCH OF THE POPCORN THAT THEY HAVE NO ROOM FOR THE TURKEY.

★ 1 quart freshly popped popcorn

FOR THE MIX

★ 3 tablespoons redcurrant jelly
★ 1 tablespoon orange juice
★ grated rind of 1 small orange
★ 1-2 tablespoons port
★ 1 tablespoon freshly chopped mint

Pop the popcorn in a large heavy-bottomed pan as previously described, just before required.

Heat the redcurrant jelly in a large pan with the orange juice and rind, stirring frequently with a wooden spoon until smooth.

Bring to a boil, and boil for 1 minute. Remove from the heat, and stir in the port and mint. Remove from the heat, and let cool slightly.

Add the freshly popped popcorn to the pan.

Stir gently with a wooden spoon until the popcorn is lightly coated. Let cool before serving in small bowls.

APRICOT AND ALMOND DELIGHTS

USE THE BEST QUALITY CONSERVE YOU CAN BUY FOR THIS RECIPE. YOU CERTAINLY WON'T REGRET IT.

★ 1 quart freshly popped popcorn

FOR THE MIX

★ 4 tablespoons apricot conserve
★ a few drops of almond extract
★ 1 tablespoon lemon juice
★ $1/2$ cup whole blanched almonds, cut into slivers

Pop the popcorn in a large heavy-bottomed pan as previously described, just before required.

If the conserve has large pieces of fruit in it, chop into bite-sized pieces, then place the conserve with the lemon juice and almond extract in a large pan.

Heat through gently, stirring occasionally until smooth. Remove from the heat, and let cool slightly.

Add the slivered almonds and freshly popped popcorn. Stir with a wooden spoon until the popcorn is completely coated.

Place in serving bowls, and eat on the same day. If desired, some chopped no-need-to-soak apricots can be added as well for an extra fruity snack.

65

BRANDIED CHOCOLATE CHERRY CORN

LOOK OUT FOR THE NATURAL CANDIED CHERRIES WHEN MAKING THIS. WASH AND DRY THE CHERRIES THOROUGHLY BEFORE ADDING TO THE MIX.

★ 1 quart freshly popped popcorn

FOR THE MIX

★ 4 squares dark chocolate
★ 2 tablespoons butter

★ 2 tablespoons brandy
★ 2 tablespoons heavy cream
★ $\frac{3}{4}$ cup whole candied cherries

Pop the popcorn in a large heavy-bottomed pan as previously described, just before required.

Break the chocolate into small pieces, and place in a heavy-bottomed pan, together with the butter and brandy.

Heat gently until the chocolate has melted, stirring occasionally with a wooden spoon. Remove from the heat, and stir in the cream.

Add the freshly popped popcorn and the cherries. Stir until the popcorn is completely coated. Let cool before serving. Eat on the same day.

66

HONEY KISSES

THERE ARE MANY VARIETIES OF HONEY AVAILABLE THESE
DAYS VARYING FROM FRAGRANT AND FLOWERY TO DARK RICH, SMOKY
FLAVORS. CHOOSE ONE WITH A PRONOUNCED FLAVOR.

★ 1 quart freshly popped popcorn

FOR THE MIX

★ 2 tablespoons butter

★ 4 tablespoons Mexican or
  similar honey
★ 1 tablespoon light corn syrup
★ 1 tablespoon shredded coconut

Pop the popcorn in a large heavy-bottomed pan as previously described, just before required.

Pour the honey into a large pan, and add the butter and syrup. Place over a gentle heat, and heat through, stirring occasionally until the butter has melted. Bring to a boil, and boil steadily for 1 minute. Remove from the heat, and let cool slightly. Then stir in the shredded coconut and freshly popped popcorn.

Stir until the popcorn is completely coated, then place in a container. Eat on the same day.

68

ROCKY MOUNTAINS

THIS POPCORN WILL BE A WINNER FOR ALL MAPLE SYRUP FANS. ADD WHATEVER FRUIT OR NUTS YOU FANCY AND MUNCH AWAY TO YOUR HEART'S CONTENT.

★ 1 quart freshly popped popcorn

FOR THE MIX

★ 4 tablespoons maple syrup

★ 2 tablespoons butter
★ ¹/₂ cup shelled, whole hazelnuts
★ ¹/₂ cup mixed cut peel

Pop the popcorn in a large heavy-bottomed pan as previously described, just before required.

Pour the maple syrup into a large pan, and add the butter. Heat through, stirring occasionally until the syrup and butter are blended. Bring to a boil, and boil for 1 minute.

Remove from the heat, and stir in the nuts, mixed peel and freshly popped popcorn. Stir until the popcorn is completely coated. Place in a container, and let cool before serving.

Chapter Five
5

fun
recipes

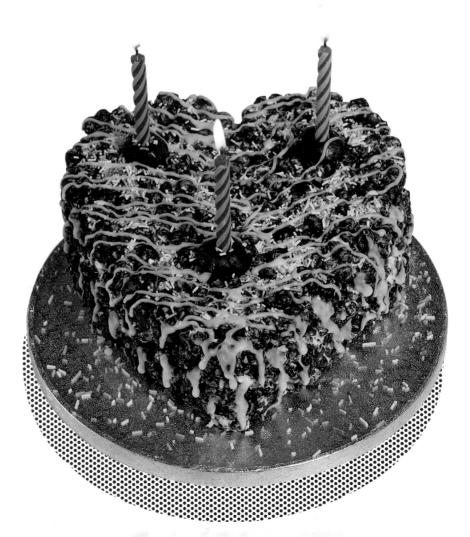

WAKEY WAKEY

START THE DAY WITH A SMILE BY EATING THIS POPCORN MUESLI. APART FROM BEING REALLY TASTY, IT'S ALSO VERY HEALTHY.

- ★ $1\frac{1}{2}$ cups freshly popped popcorn
- ★ $\frac{1}{3}$ cup rolled oats
- ★ $\frac{1}{3}$ cup raisins
- ★ $\frac{1}{2}$ cup toasted slivered almonds
- ★ $\frac{1}{2}$ cup chopped no-need-to-soak apricots
- ★ 2 bananas, sliced
- ★ $\frac{1}{2}$ cup halved seedless grapes
- ★ natural yogurt, to serve

Mix together the freshly popped popcorn, oats, raisins, almonds and apricots. (This can be done the night before and the muesli kept in an airtight container.)

When ready to eat, add the bananas and grapes, top with the yogurt and serve.

MAYO MAGIC

You can of course use either homemade or purchased mayonnaise, whichever you prefer. Try varying the flavor of the mayonnaise by adding some grated lemon or orange rind.

★ 1 quart freshly popped popcorn

FOR THE TOPPING

★ $2/3$ cup prepared mayonnaise
★ 1-2 red Fresno chili peppers, deseeded and finely chopped
★ 1 carrot, peeled and grated
★ $1/3$ cup raisins
★ 2 tablespoons freshly chopped cilantro

★ salt and freshly ground black pepper

TO SERVE

★ $1/2$ medium head red cabbage, outer leaves and central core discarded, washed thoroughly and drained
★ 4 ounces thinly sliced ham, formed into rolls

Pop the popcorn in a large heavy-bottomed pan as previously described, just before required.

Place the mayonnaise in a bowl, and stir in the chilies, carrot, raisins and cilantro. Season to taste, and mix into the freshly popped popcorn.

Shred the red cabbage finely, and arrange on a serving platter. Arrange the ham rolls around the edge. Top with the freshly popped popcorn, and serve immediately.

73

POPCORN KRISPIES

These little chocolate cakes are a big hit for all kids. Make two batches as one certainly won't be enough.

MAKES ABOUT 8

★ 1 quart freshly popped popcorn
★ 3 tablespoons light corn syrup
★ 3 squares milk chocolate, broken into pieces

★ 1 rounded tablespoon sifted cocoa powder
★ 2 tablespoons butter
★ 1 teaspoon vanilla extract

Pop the popcorn in a large heavy-bottomed pan as previously described, just before required.

Heat the syrup, chocolate, cocoa powder and butter in a large pan, stirring occasionally. When the mixture has melted, stir until smooth, then remove from the heat. Add the vanilla extract and freshly popped popcorn, and spoon into small paper cases. Leave until cold before serving.

POPCORN BIRTHDAY CAKE

IF A FUN-SHAPED MOLD IS UNAVAILABLE, DRAW A SHAPE ONTO A PIECE OF BAKING PARCHMENT PLACED ON A BAKING SHEET. SPREAD THE PREPARED POPCORN WITHIN THE SHAPE.

- ★ 2 quarts freshly popped popcorn
- ★ 4 tablespoons crunchy peanut butter
- ★ 4 squares milk chocolate
- ★ 1 rounded tablespoon sifted cocoa powder
- ★ 6 tablespoons light corn syrup
- ★ 2-3 tablespoons heavy cream
- ★ 1 cup sifted confectioners' sugar
- ★ candied cherries, angelica and birthday candles, to decorate

Lightly oil a 9-inch cake pan or mold shaped in the form of a car, rabbit or similar.

Pop the popcorn in a large heavy-bottomed pan as previously described, and reserve.

Place the peanut butter, chocolate, cocoa powder and syrup in a large heavy-bottomed pan, and heat, stirring occasionally, until smooth and well blended.

Bring to a boil, and simmer for 1 minute. Remove from the heat, and stir in the cream. Heat for 30 seconds, then remove from the heat.

Add the freshly popped popcorn, and stir until the popcorn is completely coated. Press into the lightly oiled pan or mold.

Leave until set, then turn out onto a silver cake board. Mix the confectioners' sugar with about 2-3 tablespoons hot water to form a coating consistency. Decorate the cake with the frosting, the cherries, angelica, and the candles.

74

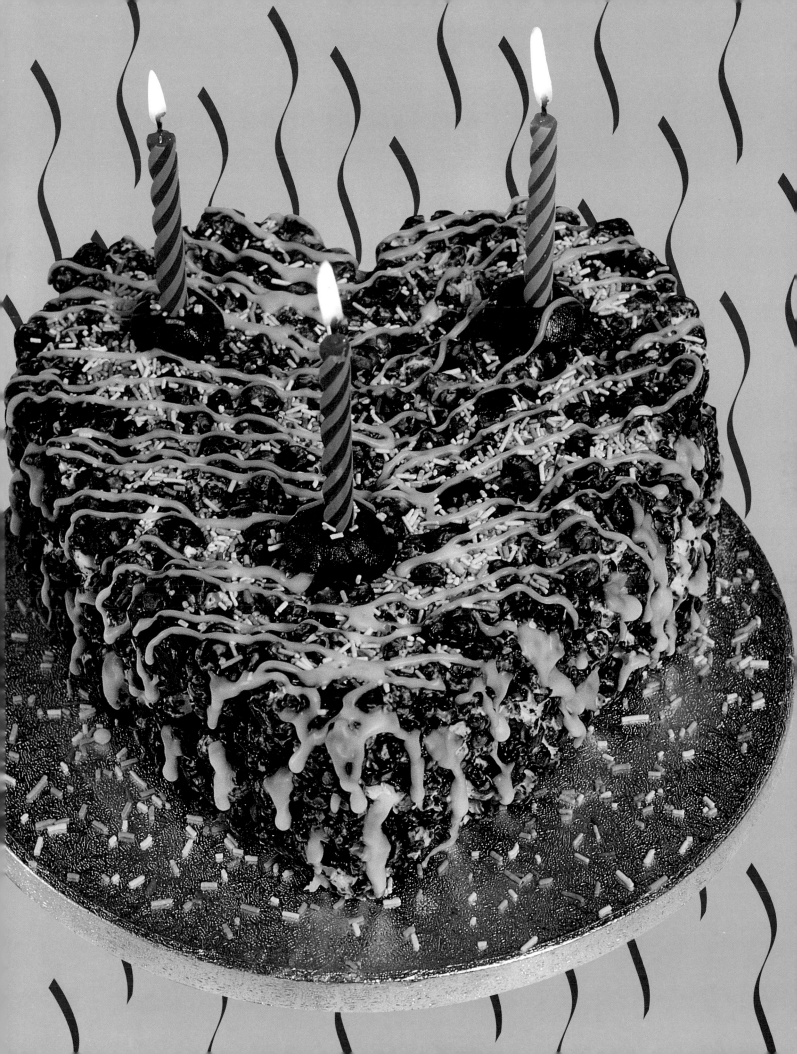

FRUITS DE MER TOPPING

**SERVE THIS AS A FUN
APPETIZER FOR AN INFORMAL LUNCH PARTY.**

★ 1 quart freshly popped
  popcorn

FOR THE TOPPING

★ 2 tablespoons olive oil
★ 1 small onion, peeled and
  chopped
★ grated rind of 1 lime
★ 1 x 7-ounce can crab meat,
  drained and flaked

★ 1 tablespoon tomato paste
★ 1 x 2-ounce can anchovy
  fillets, drained and chopped
★ 4 ounces smoked salmon,
  thinly sliced
★ 3 tablespoons prepared
  mayonnaise
★ lime wedges and strips of rind,
  to garnish

Pop the popcorn in a large heavy-bottomed pan as previously described, just before required.

Heat the oil in a pan, then sauté the onion for 5 minutes, or until soft. Remove from the heat.

Add the lime rind, flaked crab, tomato paste and chopped anchovy fillets, and mix together.

Cut the smoked salmon into thin strips, and add to the mixture, together with the mayonnaise. Stir together.

Place the freshly popped popcorn into a serving dish, and spoon over the prepared topping. Serve garnished with a lime wedge to squeeze over the seafood topping and sprinkle with strips of rind.

SWEET'N'SOUR SNAP DRAGONS

**FOR A REAL LAUGH, HAND AROUND
SOME CHOPSTICKS WITH THIS DISH, GUARANTEED TO GET ANY
PARTY GOING WITH A SWING.**

★ 1 quart freshly popped popcorn

FOR THE TOPPING

★ 2 tablespoons sunflower or corn oil
★ 1 onion, peeled and chopped
★ 1 green bell pepper, deseeded and chopped

★ 1 carrot, peeled and cut into very thin julienne strips
★ 1 x 7-ounce can pineapple
★ 1 teaspoon cornstarch
★ 1 tablespoon soy sauce
★ 1 tablespoon white wine vinegar

Pop the popcorn in a large heavy-bottomed pan as previously described, just before required.

Heat the oil in a pan, then sauté the onion and green bell pepper for 5 minutes or until soft.

Meanwhile, blanch the carrot in boiling water. Leave for 3 minutes, then drain and add to the pan.

Drain and finely chop the pineapple, reserving the juice. Add to the pan.

Blend the cornstarch with the reserved pineapple juice, the soy sauce and vinegar, and stir into the pan. Bring to a boil.

Heat, stirring continuously, until the mixture thickens, then cook for 1 minute longer. Let cool slightly.

Place the freshly popped popcorn into a serving bowl. Top with the prepared topping and serve.

POPCORN LOLLIES

**TRY PUTTING ONE OF THESE FUN LOLLIES
IN THE "TO GO" BAGS AT THE END OF A KIDS' PARTY.**

**MAKES ABOUT 4-6 DEPENDING ON
THE SIZE OF THE MOLDS.**

★ 1 quart freshly popped popcorn
★ 8 ounces plain toffees
★ 2 tablespoons milk
★ 2 tablespoons butter
★ 1 teaspoon vanilla extract

Pop the popcorn in a large heavy-bottomed pan as previously described, just before required.

Unwrap the toffees, and place in a heavy-bottomed pan, together with the milk, butter, and the vanilla extract.

Heat gently, stirring occasionally, until the toffees have melted.

Remove from the heat, and let cool slightly. Stir in the freshly popped popcorn.

Leave until cool enough to handle, then spoon into lightly-oiled lolly molds, and place the sticks in position. Leave until set before removing.

STRAWBERRY SUNDAE

**TRY THIS FUN DESSERT IN THE SUMMER
WHEN STRAWBERRIES ARE PLENTIFUL. IN THE WINTER, USE CHOPPED
CANNED FRUIT OR SEEDLESS GRAPES.**

* $1^1/_2$ cups freshly popped popcorn
* 3 tablespoons strawberry jam
* 1 tablespoon lemon juice

* 3 cups fresh strawberries, hulled and cut in half if large
* scoops of vanilla ice cream

Pop the popcorn in a large heavy-bottomed pan as previously described, just before required.

Heat the jam with the lemon juice, and stir until smooth. Remove from the heat, and let cool slightly.

Stir in the freshly popped popcorn, and mix gently until well coated.

Layer the popcorn, strawberries and ice cream in tall sundae glasses, and top with a final scoop of ice cream.

Decorate sundaes with a few pieces of popcorn and leftover strawberries.

79

INDEX